To Fr. Scott Bullock

ABOUT THE AUTHOR

JON LEONETTI is a Catholic speaker, best-selling author and radio host who conveys a message of lasting fulfillment in Jesus Christ. Through Jon's keynote presentations and parish missions, thousands of Catholics each year discover the freedom Christ offers by way of his life and love.

Jon's two books—*Mission Of The Family* and *Your God Is Too Boring*—are published and featured in Matthew Kelly's Dynamic Catholic book program. They have been endorsed by Archbishop Joseph E. Kurtz; the president of the U.S. Conference of Catholic Bishops, Mark Hart, Immaculee Ilibagiza, Brandon Vogt and more.

Jon believes that our deepest longing for happiness and wholeness is fulfilled in the encounter with Jesus Christ. Through prayer, the Sacraments, family life, and the help of Mary and the saints, Jon wants to cultivate an intimate relationship with Jesus, and help others do the same.

With this message Jon has been featured and interviewed by the nations top Catholic websites, blogs and radio shows, helping Catholics in all walks of life to fall in love and stay in love with the living God.

At home, Jon enjoys reading, sports, exercising, coffee and, most of all, spending time with his wife Teresa and children Joseph and Gianna.

INTRODUCTION:
THE GREATEST TEACHERS I'VE NEVER KNOWN

Some of the best teachers I have ever had are people I've never met, and I suspect the same is true for you. Don't believe me? How many of us learned the alphabet or how to count from *Mr. Rogers* or *Sesame Street?* I don't know about you, but I never got a chance to meet either Fred Rogers or Jim Henson (both of whom were devout Christians, by the way). Most of us learned about good and evil, virtue and vice, courage and chickening out from fairy tales, but none of us have met the Grimm Brothers or Hans Christian Andersen. Even as grown-ups in our respective fields, we seldom have a chance to meet those whose life, work, and research makes our life and our work possible. But these teachers remain really important to us; it's the reason we keep pictures of them in our offices or post their quotes to Facebook or Pinterest. It's why we keep their books on our shelves and go back to them again and again, or why we reread and retell their stories—because they inspire us to go and do likewise.

That's what culture is ultimately all about. We collect the best of what has gone before us in terms of art, science, history, or whatever, and we make it viable and creative and new and riff off of it today. It prevents us from having to reinvent the wheel in every generation, and allows us to learn from and even improve upon that which went before us. That's why G.K. Chesterton called tradition the "democracy of the dead," because it means "giving a vote to the most obscure of all classes, our ancestors."[1] In other words, we're supposed to learn from other people, and some of the people with the best ideas are going to be people we never get a chance to meet.

The Catholic Church has a special insight about these people. In the creed we say we believe in the "Communion of Saints". Now this means not just people who have been formally canonized by the Church, but all those in Heaven. And while it's certainly possible to have some really good ideas and turn out a really rotten person, or to be an excellent teacher and not wind up in Heaven, it seems safe to say that many of those who have been great teachers for us are "saints" in the broad sense. Probably many of your favorite authors fall into this category; I know that many of mine do. But the Church's teaching on the Communion of Saints presses us a step further. It reminds us that the bonds which unite Christians extend beyond the grave, which is why we pray for the intercession of the saints—both canonized and the never-gonna-be-canonized. In fact, the only way that a person ever gets canonized as a saint is because someone else prayed to them first—asked their intercession in a serious difficulty, and experienced a miracle impossible to explain without the other person's intervention. So most of us pray to the "saints" in our families too, not because we believe that Grandma and Grandpa are necessarily going to be in stained glass windows someday, but because we live in the hope that they are in Heaven, and we pray that in Heaven they will continue to do good work for us here

---

[1]   G.K. Chesterton, *Orthodoxy*. (New York: Dover Thrift Publications, 2012): 39.

on Earth. So, likewise, when you pick up a book by or about J.R.R. Tolkien, or Graham Greene, or Shusako Endo, or Flannery O'Connor, say a little prayer and ask for their intercession, that you might have the grace to see what they were really saying, and that you might take whatever good God has in store for you from that particular book.

The Church presses us even further, though. Saints are not *just* good for a little power boost of grace when we remember to ask for their prayers. Their more fundamental purpose is to urge us on, by word and example, so that we might do what they did, which means it's possible, right here and now, to have a *relationship* with the greatest teachers you've never met. You don't just have to think hard about what they wrote to get inside their head; just ask them, spend time with them, and prayerfully read what they've written to obtain the graces God has in store for you through this precious saint of His.

This is what happened to me with the greatest of teachers I have never known. You see, Mother Teresa died when I was still in grade school, and while I'm sure that I knew who she was beforehand and definitely had a sense that someone important passed away, I didn't really learn from Mother Teresa until much, much later. Now that I have come to know her, my love has grown, both for her and for Jesus, which is really the point, after all.

So, as you start this book pray with me for the intercession of Mother Teresa.

This book was a labor of love and of prayer. Read it in the same spirit, and strive not only to learn new things *about* Mother Teresa, but to get to *know* her, to grow in *love* for her and about her, and, most importantly, grow closer to the One she loved more than all else, Jesus Christ.

PRAYER

Mother Teresa,
In the midst of great weakness our God gave you great
strength,
and in serving the poorest of the poor, you found
yourself quenching the thirst of Jesus and each day
drawing closer to His own Sacred Heart.
Obtain for me, from Jesus, your love, the graces
necessary for my salvation, and in particular that in
studying your life and work I might imitate your virtues,
and especially that which I need most at this time. (Here
mention aloud or silently any particular intention,
especially whatever is getting in the way of your
spiritual growth).

O Lord, grant me the grace to persevere under stress,
even when I can no longer sense your presence, and to
love you with all of my heart, especially when it is hard
to know and feel your own love. And help me to grow
into the faithfulness which Mother Teresa showed here
on Earth, that I might be happy with her and with all
your saints forever in Heaven.

Amen.

MEMORIES OF A SAINT

I can't tell you when I first encountered Mother Teresa of Calcutta. What I do know is that she was such a dynamic figure on the world scene by the time I was born that I don't remember a time when I didn't know who she was. My first memories of her are as a frail-looking woman on the evening news, who seemed to periodically get audiences with world leaders and lovingly but firmly tell them what they were doing wrong. I do remember when she died, mostly because it was a big deal at school. I even remember watching at least part of the funeral, but, more than that, for weeks there were projects and reports and other activities involving her life. Not much of it stuck at the time, but I do remember recognizing even then, at like twelve years old, that this lady *mattered*.

I remember seeing a picture of her once; it might have been in those days following her death, or it might have been sometime later. It's of Mother Teresa and of President and Mrs. Reagan. Nancy Reagan towered over Mother, and Mrs. Reagan was only five feet four. Yet Mother Teresa is clearly the alpha in that picture. I mean, sure, Ronald Reagan could start a nuclear war with the push of a button, and Nancy Reagan got to hobnob regularly with all the leaders of the free world, but in the photo, *they* are visibly in awe of *her*. You actually get the feeling that they posed for this picture because they wanted people to know they met Mother Teresa. You definitely don't get the feeling that Mother Teresa needed everybody to know that she met the Reagans. Whenever I see that picture I'm reminded of what true power really looks like.

Mother Teresa didn't become a very important part of my life until much, much later. I was in the college seminary in Dubuque, and the rector at the time was one of the finest priests I've ever had the opportunity to know—Fr. Scott Bullock. I wanted to be this guy when I grew up. As a seminarian himself, studying in Rome, he'd had the opportunity to meet Mother Teresa. Vicariously, through a kind of divine trickle-down effect, it likewise has had a major impact on me.

As he tells the story, one day he and another seminarian decided to stop by the Missionaries of Charity chapel. In they walked, and, as he describes it, "There she was, the Famous One, sitting in the middle of the chapel alone praying." Half a dozen or so other people lined the edges of the chapel, but she knelt alone in the middle, hunched over and praying to God. He got gutsy, turned to his friend and told him he was going to go and sit by her; his friend was not so gutsy. So, the priest-to-be-Fr. Scott went and sat down by Mother Teresa and began to pray. Not long after he closed his eyes, he felt a nudge on his shoulder. Fr. Scott was preparing himself for the words that would change his life. What she said was this:

"You can't sit here! This is for the sisters!"

Mother taught humility hard and fast.

And though those words were not the kind that he was expecting, they've had a lasting and positive impact on him for years to come. He jokes about it now, but has made mention on a number of occasions of the inspiration he gained that day from staring into the eyes of someone so ordered and disciplined for God.

LIFE AND DEATH

Clearly you know who Mother Teresa was, or you wouldn't be reading this book.

But I'm not here to tell you about who she *was,* I want you to know who she *is,* because her God and ours is "the God, not of the dead, but of the living; because to Him all are alive."[2]

Of course, in order to show you who she is today, I do have to tell something of the story of her life and how she became the woman we all know about. Now, you may think you know her story, and maybe you do. Some of you may even know the nuts and bolts of her life— the Wikipedia entry, if you will—much better than I do. But for the next few minutes, pretend that you're hearing it all for the very first time. Let me paint a picture or set a scene for you, because none of us are as simple as we seem to be, and it may well be that you didn't know the Queen of the Streets of Calcutta as well as you thought you did.

Once upon a time, far up in the Himalayan foothills, lay the beautiful town of Darjeeling. And living there in Darjeeling was a little wisp of a woman with a name

---

[2]   Luke 20:37 (NAB)

you couldn't hope to pronounce—Anjezë Gonxhe Bojaxhiu. Anjezë was tiny and frail, it looked as if a stiff breeze could blow her away, and she was only nineteen years old. She had come to India from her native Albania to be a missionary.

When she took her religious vows, she took the name Teresa, after St. Thérèse of Lisieux, the new patron saint of missionaries (St. Thérèse had herself been canonized just a couple of years before, and was also a sickly young woman whom no one thought would amount to very much). Another one of the sisters had already taken the name Thérèse though, so Teresa adopted the Spanish spelling, which usually refers to St. Teresa of Avila. In surprising ways she came to emulate both women, far more than anyone in 1928 could begin to imagine.

Darjeeling was a very comfortable place to be a missionary. It was, and still is, a charming little city full of clean mountain air and picturesque mountain views. It stands a mile high up in the Himalayan Mountains, surrounded by the elegant estates that produce the world famous Darjeeling tea (the champagne of teas!). Everything about the town is scenic, including the narrow-gauge train that leads into and out of the town, which is still today pulled by a huffing little steam locomotive that looks for all the world like a life-sized children's toy.

Sister Teresa was just about the least important person in Darjeeling at the time, and no one expected anything much out of her. She served her purpose as a schoolteacher, which is what the Loreto Sisters, whom she had joined to become a missionary, had sent her to do. At first they had her teach in the convent school in Darjeeling, but eventually she was moved from Darjeeling to Calcutta, and that would change everything—*everything*.

As it turned out, the young nun from Albania arrived just in time for some of the worst years of Indian history. India in the 1940s suffered far more than most Westerners realize—and especially Calcutta. The Japanese invasion of Burma and other British possessions in East Asia sent thousands of refugees flooding into Calcutta. Then Calcutta itself was bombed—there wasn't all that much damage, compared to what happened to other cities during the war, but thousands of refugees fled the city with nowhere else to go. And then, in 1943, there was a famine that killed thousands—not mainly affecting the poorest of the poor, as you might expect, but mostly craftsmen and their families, who starved when their customers stopped spending money on anything but food. It was a horrible situation, difficult for the young sister to imagine things getting much harder.

And then the war ended, and things got much, much worse—far worse than anyone could have predicted.

1946 was a momentous year in Indian history: frightening, enlightening, passion-stirring, and challenging. With the war ended at last, the British were working toward giving India independence. *But what was India?* For the British, India was the vast subcontinent that ran from the Himalayas south, beyond the valley of the Indus in the west to beyond the valley of the Ganges in the east. The British had pieced together this vast empire from more than five hundred different states, with more different languages than in all of Europe combined. Most of central India was Hindu, but there were large Muslim majorities in the western and eastern parts. The British plan was to make all of India one vast nation. But the Muslims were worried that the large Hindu majority would begin to oppress the Muslim minority without the British colonial government to protect them. The Muslim League was formed to insist on a separate nation specifically for Indian Muslims—the nation we now know as Pakistan.

Mahatma Gandhi, the great leader in the struggle for Indian independence, had always insisted on nonviolence as the way to achieve any goal. He believed strongly that Hindus, Muslims, Sikhs, and Christians in India could all live together peacefully, and the overwhelming majority of the Indian population agreed. Even still, all through 1946, vile propaganda from both sides spread the same message of terror in newspapers and on the radio: Hindus and Muslims can never live in peace.

The Muslim League called for a day of peaceful protest on August 16. But what happened was anything but peaceful. With months of toxic rhetoric coming from both sides, the country exploded into unbelievable horror, and the heart of the explosion was downtown Calcutta. In just three days of rage-fueled riots more than 4,000 people were killed—Hindus and Muslims alike—and more than 100,000 left homeless.

This was the Calcutta that Sister Teresa came to know in the late summer of 1946. It was a city filled with violence, misery, and homelessness. When, less than a month after all the riots and killings, she got on a train headed out of the city, most of us would have been thinking of leaving for good. Not Sister Teresa, however; something else was already stirring inside her head and her heart.

Despite poor health and general frailty, the young sister had been successful at everything she'd been asked to do. She was a well-respected teacher in Darjeeling, and accomplished enough once she moved to Calcutta that she was appointed the headmistress in 1944. She'd shown herself again and again not only to be a very fine teacher, but an able administrator as well.

Now, I suspect that if you or I had boarded that train out of Calcutta in the late summer of 1946, it would have been to get out of India as fast as the tracks could carry us. Or at least we'd have been happy to be going back to Darjeeling—out of the heat, starvation, and death that was Calcutta, up into the clean mountain air and luxurious views. Darjeeling would have been an easy escape—a welcome and entirely understandable haven far from the misery of the city below.

But something remarkable happened on that train.

Teresa could never really describe it in words. Afterwards, she told the sisters that she had been given a *call within a call*—a mission to serve the poorest of the poor. She only hinted at what the experience had been like: an overwhelming sense of the presence of God filling her entire being. She always spoke of September 10 as "Inspiration Day." But she didn't like to talk about the details of what she had experienced. She knew, though, that Jesus had come to her directly—and given her a very specific assignment. "Will you do this for me?" Jesus asked her.

How could she say no?

By the time she reached Darjeeling, her whole life had changed. She knew that she wasn't going to spend the rest of her life as a comfortable headmistress in a privileged Catholic school; not that she wasn't doing good work as a teacher, but now she had a mission that was bigger than that. It was a mission to serve Christ directly, because now she truly understood that each of those faces she saw on the street—the dying beggar, the homeless child, the weeping leper—was the face of Christ Himself. "He makes himself the hungry one—the naked one—the homeless one—the sick one—the one in prison—the lonely one—the unwanted one—and he says: You did it to me."[3]

He did say something about that Himself, after all:

> Then the King will say to those at his right hand, "Come, O blessed of my Father, inherit the

---

[3]   Mother Teresa, Nobel Lecture. 11 December 1979. http://www.nobelprize.org/nobel_prizes/peace/laureates/1979/teresa-lecture.html

kingdom prepared for you from the foundation of the world; for I was hungry and you gave me food, I was thirsty and you gave me drink, I was a stranger and you welcomed me, I was naked and you clothed me, I was sick and you visited me, I was in prison and you came to me"

Then the righteous will answer him, "Lord, when did we see you hungry and feed you, or thirsty and give you drink? And when did we see you a stranger and welcome you, or naked and clothe you? And when did we see you sick or in prison and visit you?"

And the King will answer them, "Truly, I say to you, as you did it to one of the least of these my brethren, you did it to me."[4]

This is, of course, the mission that Jesus gives to every Christian. But that day on that train ride, Sister Teresa felt its depth. Whatever happened to her while riding the train that day, she would spend the rest of her life living it out—showing the world what it meant to take Christ at His word—answering that *call within a call*.

It took her more than a year to get the mission going, and she wouldn't let any roadblocks stand in her way. By 1948, she was out in the streets of Calcutta, doing the work she knew God had made her to do. She took some basic medical training, so she could help the sick when they had no other means of help. She became a

---

[4]   Matthew 25:34-40 (NAB)

citizen of her new and adopted nation of India. Instead of the habit of the Sisters of Loreto, she wore a traditional Indian sari with a blue border she had designed herself. She became one of the people she had come to serve.

This new work she had chosen for herself—what she discerned God had truly chosen for her, had made her for—was very, very difficult. "The poverty of the poor must be so hard for them," she wrote in her diary. "While looking for a home I walked and walked until my arms and my legs ached." At this early stage, when she was first experiencing such radical poverty on a personal level, she had trouble identifying herself with those she served. "I thought how much they [the poor] must ache in body and soul, looking for a home, food and health."[5] There was, in the beginning, still an "us" and a "them", fueled, no doubt, in part by the sometimes chilly reception she received from the locals. But Teresa's compassion was no mere sympathetic nod from a rich socialite. She had put herself in the place of the poor, and it wasn't until she came to identify with her poverty that she was able to truly live freely.

Things were desperate in those days, and because she refused to rely on any more charity than the poor whom she was serving, she had to beg not only for her own food and housing, but for supplies, medicine, and everything she needed for the mission. She had no car, and couldn't afford to spend money on the crowded and

[5]   Reprinted in *Nobel's Women of Peace*. Edited by Michelle Benjamin. (Toronto: Second Story Press, 2008): 12.

stifling trams. So she walked everywhere, until every bone in her body hurt.

It would have been so easy to go back to the Sisters of Loreto. They were, after all, the women who had formed her in religious life, taught her how to be a nun, women with whom she had lived and worked and prayed for more than fifteen years. And to return would simply have meant that her little experiment in social services hadn't worked. Teresa did her best, but no one came through with the funds. Moreover, the Sisters of Loreto had a different purpose in the Church and in the world, and she had vowed herself to them first. No one would blame her for returning—not one.

Except, of course, Teresa herself. She was convinced that those thoughts came from the devil, tempting her with visions of the comforts of the convent she had left behind. "'You have only to say the word and all that will be yours again,' the Tempter kept on saying." But she would not be tempted. She prayed to God, telling Him she was ready to do His will, whatever it was, and whatever would come of it.

And soon the lonely work began to pay off. By 1950, she had a group of dedicated followers—thirteen of them—that was officially established as the *Missionaries of Charity*. A totally new religious congregation (not based on some pre-existing order) hadn't been approved by Rome in more than one hundred years, but Teresa's character was so striking, and the way that she and her sisters lived their lives of prayer and service so compelling, that Church authorities realized that to get in the way of the Little Nun from Calcutta would be to inhibit the work of Christ Himself. Sister Teresa had become the mother of her own order.

People quickly learned that Mother Teresa and her sisters would go where no one else would dare to help the people whom no one else would help. The municipal authorities in Calcutta, delighted to have someone doing the work they didn't have the resources to do, donated an abandoned Hindu temple in a densely crowded city neighborhood, and there Mother Teresa opened her first Home for the Dying. It was, and still is, a very primitive place if you measure it by the standards of an American hospice. Medical care was limited to what Mother Teresa and the other members of her order could provide because there was no money to pay for doctors or even proper nurses. Medicine was what the sisters could round up or beg. But it was a place where poor people could die with dignity, knowing that there was someone nearby who cared about them. No one would die alone under Teresa's watch.

Mother Teresa soon developed something of a reputation as a taskmaster. She expected hard work from her followers—and she got it, mostly because they could see that she worked harder than anybody. The order grew quickly, and soon had hospitals for leprosy, homes for the dying, and orphanages all over India.

And this little Albanian woman in a sari had to run it all.

Of course, running big organizations is hard work all by

itself. Mother had shown herself to be a good administrator as the principal of the girls' school in Darjeeling, but nothing could have prepared her to run multiple hospitals, hospices, orphanages, and charities. The real source of hardship for Mother, however, came from a deep inner darkness. She felt empty most of the time, and any felt sense of the presence of God left her– –sometimes for years at a time. She had that one unspeakable experience on the train to Darjeeling, but ever after Mother Teresa lived in a spiritual desert. And none of her sisters knew; no one knew, really, apart from the archbishop and a handful of priests who served as her spiritual directors.

And as the years went by, she felt nothing; but she *did* something. She did the work. She *loved.* This is what I keep saying, and now I'm saying it again. Love is not a feeling. It's what you *do,* and you keep *doing* it whether the feeling is there or not. Oftentimes the real test is whether you can *do it,* even when you can't *feel it.*

This is the "greater love" that Christ spoke of, and that He showed us at the Supper and on the Cross. It's not the romantic love of popular movies, not the comfortable, cozy, family love of Christmas cards. Jesus, Mother Teresa reminded us, "died on the cross to show that greater love, and he died for you and for me and for that leper and for that man dying of hunger and that naked person lying in the street not only of Calcutta, but of Africa, and New York, and London, and Oslo... And so this is very important for us to realize that love, to be true, has to hurt. It hurt Jesus to love us, it hurt him." And so it hurt her—and she loved even harder.

That love was what was so compelling, and people responded to it whether they recognized that it came from Jesus or not. It inspired people to join Mother and work beside her, and not only other Catholics, but Hindus and Muslims as well. She accomplished in her charities what even Gandhi could not in his protests— she brought Hindus and Muslims together in a common cause: *love.* In recognition of that love Mother Teresa was granted the *Padma Shri*, one of the highest civil honors bestowed by the Government of India (think the Presidential Medal of Freedom if you're from the US).

By the early 1960s, the order was expanding outside India. By the 1970s, it was everywhere—wherever there was poverty or misery, the Missionaries of Charity were helping the poorest and most miserable. In 1979, Mother Teresa was awarded the Nobel Peace Prize—because, as the awards committee said, "poverty and distress are also threats to peace." Mother was hesitant about receiving the award, and especially the cost incurred in making the trip to receive it, but she eventually agreed when her advisors convinced her that accepting the prize would provide the opportunity to highlight the plight of the poor on a global scale. There's usually a lavish dinner when the prize is awarded, but Mother Teresa asked that the money be spent on the poor of India instead.

So Mother Teresa became an international celebrity, just by doing what she knew she had to do. She didn't really look for celebrity—in fact, she actively worked against it—but when it became clear that notoriety was going to be hers whether she wanted it or not, she made sure to put it to good use. It got her into places no one else could get into, and certainly not nuns who ran soup kitchens in underprivileged countries. When she heard that there were dozens of children trapped in a hospital on the front lines during the siege of Beirut in 1982, she did what no one else could do—she managed to get the Israeli and Palestinian forces to agree to a temporary ceasefire long enough for her to go in personally with the Red Cross and bring the children out. This is just one story, but there are dozens, probably hundreds, of individual interventions that Mother made on behalf of those who could not help themselves.

Mother Teresa wasn't a hero for everyone, however. Some people in India resented her: they thought she ran her charities only as a front for forcing conversions to Christianity. Doctors from Western nations criticized conditions at her home for the dying in Calcutta—comparing them to the standards in Western hospices, rather than the genuine alternative, which was no care at all and dying in the streets. And, of course, she offended most "sophisticated" Westerners by taking a strictly Catholic line on abortion. "Today," she said when she accepted the Nobel prize, "the greatest destroyer of peace is abortion." There must have been a lot of prosperous Norwegians squirming when she said that.

Obviously Mother Teresa's success was the work of God—and really the surest sign to her that she was, in fact, doing God's will—but it was also the result of a lot of blood, sweat, and tears on her part. And this success came at a price. Mother Teresa wore herself out—not just once, but repeatedly. In 1983, she had a heart attack. In 1989, she had another. She caught pneumonia in Mexico in 1991, and that resulted in yet more permanent damage to her heart. She was, literally and figuratively, loving *to death.*

Faced with all these health problems, Mother Teresa offered to resign as head of the Missionaries of Charity, but the sisters wouldn't hear of it. So she kept working until, finally, in 1997, she couldn't work any longer. She stepped down as head of the order, and six months later she died. She had worked for fifty years on her mission to serve the poorest of the poor. And we know now from her own writings that most of the time she wasn't even getting the reward of good feelings from it. She knew what she had to do, and she did it; she understood from experience the meaning of the Lord's words to St. Paul: "My grace is sufficient for you." Christ had given her all she needed; it was up to her to make good on the gift.

LIFE AND AFTERLIFE

Mother Teresa is one of the few people in recent memory who was called, even in her own lifetime, a "living saint". It was no surprise then when, almost immediately upon her death, cries of "Santo subito!" or *"Sainthood now!"* arose from every corner of the world. More than a million people filed past her coffin in the week she lay in state at St. Thomas cathedral in Calcutta, and her funeral was broadcast live all over the world. Surely even then there were thousands of those gathered not only mourning her passing, but asking her prayers.

Very quickly after her death Pope John Paul II waived the automatic waiting period before the long process of canonization could begin. And, again, almost immediately reports started coming in from all over the world of miracles performed by the intercession of Mother Teresa. Some of them were frauds, others the result of pious imaginations, but some, no doubt, were true. The Holy See thought so too, which is why, in 2002, just five years after her death, she was beatified.

The miracle that led to her beatification involved the healing of a young Indian woman, Monica Basra, from an abdominal tumor. She was already undergoing several kinds of treatment, none of which seemed to be working. Then she had an experience of some kind with Mother. While visiting a Church, she said a light came from an image of Mother Teresa. That night, a madalian of Mother was placed on her stomach and at 1:00am she awoke. No more tumor. No medical explanation.

The second miracle, which has lead to her forthcoming canonization in September of 2016, also involved the healing of treatment-resistant tumors. A man, sick for two years found himself in the ICU. His wife, standing by his bedside in anquish, pulled a relic of Mother Teresa out of her pocket. The relic was given to them before their wedding and meant a great deal to them. She placed it on his head where the abscesses were and said a short prayer. You can probably guess what happened next. Now, eight years later, the once dying man tells his story. And like the first approved miracle, no medical explanation.

These are just two of the dozens, probably hundreds of miracles that people report due to Mother Teresa's intercession. The point is not that a certain number of prayers or the right kind of prayers result in a healing, but rather, that the saint continues to pray for us after death even as they had before.

What is most telling about Mother Teresa's legacy, however, is less the formal process of beatification and canonization, though obviously that's really important, but her model and witness and example have been so profound that even Hollywood has noticed. There have been two full-length films and a television miniseries devoted to her life, as well as dozens of documentaries and shorter films, many of which have won awards. New books on her life and spirituality come out every month, and she remains one of the most recognized people on the planet—twenty years after her death.

Easily the most important contribution Mother has made to the life of the Church following her death has come with the release of her letters in the book, *Come, Be My Light.* These letters reveal the inner spiritual darkness that Mother struggled with, and the temptations with which she struggled. At the time many were shocked, some even scandalized, or at least hoped that Christians would be, that perhaps the best Christian of the twentieth century went years without any consoling experiences and at times wondered whether God was there or cared. Far from scandalizing the faithful, however, these letters have only shored up people's regard for Mother Teresa personally, and have allowed her to become an important intercessor and patroness for those struggling with depression and spiritual darkness.

As in the way she lived her public life, Mother's private life is important, not because of *what* she did, but because of *how* she did it—with great, great love. Four pillars have marked her life and spirituality, at least as I have come to know her, and she in turn has come to form me. These four pillars are the basis of my relationship with Mother Teresa, and I think are probably useful starting points for you too. They are: mission, vocation, poverty, and suffering.

MISSION

Like many of the saints, Mother Teresa *of* Calcutta wasn't *from* Calcutta, any more than St. Patrick *of* Ireland was *from Ireland*. Patrick was kidnapped by pirates and sent to Ireland as a slave (another story that people don't know as well as they think they do), and Mother Teresa was *from* Albania, but was sent, after a short stay in Ireland, to teach in India. She took seriously the words announced at the end of Mass: *Ite, missa est!* This is translated colloquially as, "Go forth, the Mass is ended," but is probably better expressed as, *"Go! You are sent!"*

The young Teresa's missionary instincts may have kicked into high gear on that train ride to Darjeeling, but they'd been stirring for years.

I was only twelve years old then. I lived at home and with my parents; we children used to go to a non-Catholic school but we also had very good priests who were helping the boys and the girls to follow their vocation according to the call of God. It was then that I first knew I had a vocation to the poor.

This missionary impulse is precisely what drove her to the Loreto sisters. The Loretos had been founded in the mid-1500s precisely to be active in the apostolate; still living an authentic religious life, but unencumbered by the rigid discipline of the cloister. What the young Sister Teresa experienced, however, first in Dublin and then later in Darjeeling, was a kind of half-cloistered existence which revolved mostly around educating the children of the privileged classes. Though she loved her time there, and especially the sisters and students she knew from her life as a Loreto Sister, it should not come as a surprise that one who had such a strong missionary impulse so young would find running a boarding school didn't satisfy her deeper longing.

This sense of mission was at the heart of her new work. It's no accident that she named her new congregation the *Missionaries* of Charity. They were not to be called the *Teresians* (though in fairness here, none of the great founders of religious orders ever named their orders after themselves—that always came later). She saw Mary, the Blessed Virgin, as the "first Missionary of Charity". This is because:

I think none of you have realized the most wonderful part of the mission of our Society...The Society is dedicated to the Immaculate Heart of Mary...Mary is the first person in the whole of creation who received Jesus physically in her body and she is the one to carry Jesus to John... She went in haste. She is the first one to nurse Him, to clothe Him, to feed Him, to look after Him, to take care of Him, to teach Him...That is why she is the first MC—the carrier of God's love—and we, like her, do what she did: receive Jesus and give Him in haste.

Mother Teresa both anticipated and put into practice the vision of missionary activity promoted by Vatican II.

The pilgrim Church is missionary by her very nature, since it is from the mission of the Son and the mission of the Holy Spirit that she draws her origin, in accordance with the decree of God the Father.

As far as Mother Teresa was concerned, what it meant to be a Christian was to be a missionary.

VOCATION

It would be easy to imagine that Mother Teresa's success and the staggering growth of the Missionaries of Charity was because Mother had a great idea and was a really good administrator who put that idea into action. As far as Mother was concerned, the success of her mission was due *entirely,* not in part or a little bit, but *entirely* to the fact that it was not her idea to start off with. Whether you believe that or not, it's important that she did, because it stands at the heart of what the Church means when it talks about "vocation".

Most of us think of "vocations" as either: A) Pitching for priesthood or religious life; or B) Figuring out whether we should be married, single, priests, or religious. But the truth is a whole lot more complicated than that. The word "vocation" comes from the Latin *vocare*, meaning "to call". Vocations are genuine callings from God, invitations *from God* to particular ways of living and working out the Christian life. Of course, the main way that most of us do that is as married Christians, single folk, priests, or religious, but if we turn vocations and discernment simply into career counseling for churchy people then we've mistaken the point.

I spent a lot of time in my early adulthood believing that God wanted me to be a priest. I studied in seminaries, went to all sorts of conferences, workshops, and activities, read every book I could on the priesthood, and spent much of my own time alone with the Lord in prayer trying to work this out. Eventually, I did. And just 10 months after leaving the seminary, I met my wife, Teresa. And wouldn't you know it, but after meeting Teresa a whole lot of things started to fall into place and make sense about my life previously. More importantly, in my life with Teresa (my wife, not the Mother of Calcutta), I have grown more, been challenged more, and prayed more, than all of my time in seminary, and more than I probably would have ever managed as a priest.

Which is not to say it felt like it at the time. I remember
agonizing over this with friends, especially priest friends
and fellow seminarians who knew me well. But in the
end I could not shake the conviction that *God* had put
Teresa in my life, and that to turn my back on that gift
would be to reject the most precious grace I'd ever been
given. It wasn't that I *couldn't* refuse; I just didn't want
to anymore, because I wasn't confused anymore. I *knew*
deep down in my bones what I had to do, and I was free
and glad to do it.

Now, it would be easy to think, *"Mother Teresa's a holy
woman. Discernment must have been easy for her,"* but
if you still do, go back and read the first part of this little
book. Discernment was really, really hard for her. It
took her sixteen years *after entering the convent* to
figure out what God really had in mind for her to do,
and in order to do it that meant letting go of a lot—what
she had, who she thought she was, and who everyone
else thought she ought to be.

If you didn't get it from the short bio, let me spell it out
for you: one of the greatest challenges of Mother's life
was leaving the Sisters of Loreto to found her own
order. For those of us who aren't religious or don't hang
around religious very much, this might seem like it's not
a very big deal, like working for Pepsi and going to
work for Coca-Cola. But it wasn't. It was much more
difficult.

She'd spent her entire adult life with the Loretos, living

and working and praying, and they'd taught her what it meant to be a religious sister. Now she was leaving them, not to stop being a sister, but to be a sister in a very different way than they were, and that had to be very scary, both for her and for them. She wrote as much herself: "To leave Loreto was my greatest sacrifice, the most difficult thing I have ever done. It was much more difficult than to leave my family and country to enter religious life."

The key, I think, to understanding how Mother Teresa was able to get through this, and how she was able to make sense for herself of the sacrifice involved in starting her new mission, is the language she used to talk about the experience on the train. Whenever she talked about the experience, which made her visibly uncomfortable and was obviously very difficult to describe, she spoke of it as a "call within a call". She was not so much renouncing her former way of life as embracing a new way of living the same life, the same vows, the same vocation. This is why, in one of her rare statements about herself, she said:

> By birth I am Albanian. I am an Indian citizen. I am a Catholic nun. In what I do, I belong to the whole world, but my heart belongs entirely to Jesus.

A vocation, any genuine vocation, is about *how* we belong to *Jesus.* The genius of Mother Teresa's insight here is that she recognized that we can belong to Jesus in any number of ways, and that those ways might even change throughout our lifetime. I have a priest friend who talks about this in terms of our "Big V" or "Capital V" *Vocation* and our "Little v" *vocation.* Big V Vocations are the fundamental way in which our life with Christ is lived out: as spouses, or religious, or clergy, or single people; little v vocations are the particular ways in which those Big V vocations are carried out concretely. I know that God has called me to be a husband and father. Right now He's calling me to fulfill that call by writing, speaking, and giving parish missions. At some point in my life He may well call me to a more conventional job, or give me a different kind of mission altogether. The point is that the success of our Big V vocation usually depends upon our ability to discern the Little v vocation as well—and to trust God in the little things as much as in the big things.

Everywhere I go I encounter people struggling with failed relationships, career changes, life transitions, and a sense of failure, or at least a lack of success. Mother Teresa's strong sense of vocation—that God's Providence is big enough to run the world and particular enough to direct my life—is the only thing that will ultimately satisfy this longing and calm this particular anxiety. That's the true meaning of one of her most common quotations:

"Not all of us can do great things. But we can do small things with great love."

POVERTY

There are some people who *really* hate Mother Teresa. It seems counterintuitive, right? Who can hate this tiny nun who just wanted to go around helping poor people? Well, it turns out, there are lots of people. Most fall into two camps: those who think her charity was a front for something else, and those who think she glorified poverty. Neither of them get it right, but that's because they tend not to understand Christianity in general and Catholicism in particular. Understood rightly, Mother Teresa exemplified those virtues proper to the Christian life, which is why, even during her life, people were calling her a "saint".

In her lifetime, and especially early on in her work, she was met with suspicion from local Hindus and Muslims who saw her charitable work as a thinly veiled attempt to convert vulnerable non-Christians. Despite the testimony of literally thousands of people who have been cared for in hospitals, hospices, orphanages, and other charities run by the Missionaries of Charity, this rumor persists. So constant has the charge been that the Missionaries of Charity have had to put this up on their website:

> The Constitutions of the Missionaries of Charity state: "We shall not impose our Catholic Faith on anyone, but have profound respect for all religions, for it is never lawful for anyone to force others to embrace the Catholic Faith against their conscience." This reflects the intention of Mother Teresa herself, and the Missionaries of Charity follow in her footsteps.

The other charge most frequently leveled against Mother Teresa is that she glorified poverty and had a vested interest in keeping poor people impoverished. This charge was most famously made by the English atheist Christopher Hitchens in an extended essay he wrote called "The Missionary Position: Mother Teresa in Theory and Practice". If you couldn't get it from the title, he's just trying to be offensive. Hitchens, and those who have followed in his footsteps, have shown a staggering degree of ignorance with regard to religious life in the Catholic Church, how ordinary charities actually conduct their business, and seem to want to hold Mother and the Missionaries of Charity to a standard that even they don't profess to hold. As Hitchens put it himself, "Mother Teresa is less interested in helping the poor than in using them as an indefatigable source of wretchedness on which to fuel the expansion of her fundamentalist Roman Catholic beliefs."

This criticism, whether from Hitchens or others, tends to go one of two ways. Most commonly and earlier on, people would go to India to spend time with the community. Western observers, especially from the States and the UK, were generally appalled at the state of things in the hospitals, hospices, and orphanages run by the Missionaries of Charity. They were too hot, poorly ventilated, unhygienic, and when it came to the sick and the dying, typically didn't offer what seemed to be sufficient care. The problem, of course, was that they were comparing the state of a hospital in Calcutta to a hospital in London, rather than a hospital in Calcutta to a hospital in Mumbai, or the even more realistic alternative: a mat on the streets while feebly fighting off rats.

The more serious charges have to do with Mother's overall attitude towards poverty and whether or not she glorified the suffering of the poor. It's certainly true that Mother would say things about poverty that would ruffle most contemporary western feathers, things like,"I think it is very beautiful for the poor to accept their lot, to share it with the passion of Christ. I think the world is being much helped by the suffering of the poor people." But, of course, that's not so very different than what Christ Himself had to say: "If you wish to be perfect, go, sell what you have and give to [the] poor, and you will have treasure in heaven. Then come, follow me."

The critiques leveled against Mother Teresa are similar to those often often leveled against Jesus. "Why does he eat with tax collectors and sinners?" And so her critics ask, "Why did she accept money from this crooked businessman? Why did she accept charity from this sketchy government official? In short, "Why doesn't she just do what we'd like her to do, and help the poor in a way that doesn't challenge me to change my life." Without a doubt, on that score, the thing which made her most unpopular in the US was her hardline take on abortion. "It is a poverty to decide that a child must die so that you may do as you wish."

Mother was also accused of hypocrisy because the standard of health care for her and her sisters was higher than that which they offered to those in their shelters. Mother had two heart attacks and was on heart medication for most of the latter part of her life. Hitchens and company felt that she should have passed on medical treatment since those who came into the hospitals of her order couldn't afford such care. But would we ask the same of any doctor or nurse in London or New York or Chicago? This just isn't how religious life works. In fact, religious orders are bound to see to the medical care of their members. The poverty of the religious is evangelical—for the sake of the Kingdom—not because illness, disease, and destitution are values themselves.

Nowhere is this confusion more apparent than in the infamous charge that "Mother Teresa was a friend of poverty, not the poor." That's like saying Abraham Lincoln abolished slavery but freed no slaves; it's poisonous rhetoric aimed at an emotional, rather than a rational response. There are millions, literally *millions* of poor people running around today who happily identify themselves as friends of Mother Teresa, of her sisters, and of the Church, and many of them never become Christians.

But some do, and this is why so many misunderstand Mother Teresa, her life, her work, her mission, and her continued influence today. Mother Teresa was first and foremost a Christian, a religious sister in the Roman Catholic Church. She marked her days by the saying of the Divine Office and attending Holy Mass. She spent an hour each day (at least) in adoration of the Blessed Sacrament. She ate, drank, and slept with the scriptures, went to confession every week without fail, and if she wasn't using her hands for something else, was firmly clasping a rosary. To misunderstand Mother Teresa is to misunderstand the Catholic Faith.

I'm not a social worker. I don't do it for this reason. I do it for Christ. I do it for the church.[6]

SUFFERING

It's ironic that Mother Teresa gave her whole life to alleviating the suffering of other people, but has been accused of glorifying that suffering and using it for profit. Her critics misunderstand Mother's attitude towards suffering because they misunderstand Jesus and His relationship to suffering. Mother's work was simply that of Jesus—to redeem suffering from the meaninglessness of a sinful world. She alleviated what suffering she could, but knowing that the task was beyond her, she also helped those who suffered to find meaning, strength, and dignity in their suffering. And like Jesus, she was willing to suffer alongside them. What her critics get right, however, is that you can't understand Mother apart from her attitude towards suffering and the role that it had in her own spiritual life.

"If I ever become a Saint—I will surely be one of 'darkness.'" Mother Teresa wrote these words to her spiritual director in 1959. By this point she had been busy about her new mission for more than ten years, and yet all during this time this cheerful smile and confident character held a secret, a secret too terrible and too beautiful for most of us to endure.

She wrote to another advisor just two years before

---

[6]   So, she would say, should we.

Now Father — since 49 or 50 this terrible sense of loss — this untold darkness — this loneliness this continual longing for God — which gives me that pain deep down in my heart — Darkness is such that I really do not see — neither with my mind nor with my reason — the place of God in my soul is blank — There is no God in me — when the pain of longing is so great — I just long and long for God — and then it is that I feel — He does not want me — He is not there — God does not want me — Sometimes — I just hear my own heart cry out — "My God" and nothing else comes — the torture and the pain I can't explain...[7]

From the moment her mission began enjoying true success, from the beginning when, against all odds, her community was approved as a new congregation in the Church, she *felt nothing*. There were no consolations, no moments of bliss. That thing atheists accuse us of all the time—of using God as a sort of pain-killer for a kind of salve to heal the pain that comes from living in a senseless world—simply was not possible for the woman who probably encountered the most human misery of any one person firsthand in the twentieth century. She had no warm fuzzies and no spiritual delights. And as it turned out, this would last not just for

---

[7]   Mother Teresa, *Come, Be My Light.* Edited with an Introduction by Fr. Brian Kolodiejchuk. (New York: Crown Publishing, 2007): 1-2.

the first ten years—it was her primary experience of God for the last fifty years of her life!

Now, when all of this came out in 2007 the mainstream media made a huge mess of it. There were headlines all over the place suggesting that Mother Teresa was a closet atheist, that her whole spiritual life had been a fraud, and that her attitude towards suffering and poverty was due more to mental illness than Christian faith. Of course, they misunderstood the whole thing. The letters and journal entries which contained these insights into Mother's spiritual life were published in 2007 to help mark the tenth anniversary of her death *by her own order.* Fr. Brian Kolodiejchuk, who edited the volume, is the postulator for her cause—the guy responsible for advocating for her sainthood, and a man who helped Mother found the male branches of the Missionaries of Charity. Clearly her own people weren't scandalized by her experience of darkness. In fact, once revealed, it simply gave them deeper insight into the woman they already knew and loved; if anything, it helped them to love her more.

Mother Teresa's experience of spiritual darkness puts her in the same company as many of the great mystics of the Church: St. John of the Cross, St. Teresa of Avila, St. Thomas Aquinas, and even her own namesake, St. Therese of Liseux. For those who believe, the loss of sensible consolations can actually be seen as a grace rather than a burden, because the acts of love which follow are as selfless as they come. When there is no reward, either externally or internally, then the charity is as authentic as can be. So rather than suggest anything wrong or false about Mother Teresa, the revelation of her spiritual darkness actually proves the opposite: she was the real deal, absolutely, without question, and she did it all, *all*—for love.

Mother Teresa's experience of desolation and spiritual abandonment makes her an excellent model and patron for all of those experiencing spiritual hardship themselves. When you feel abandoned by God, when you can't sense His presence anymore in your life, when you're tempted to give up because it all seems so worthless—think on the Poor Woman of Calcutta who gave it all away, and never once "felt" right again, but would do it over and over and over again, because she knew it as the right thing to do. And ask that woman to pray for you, who has suffered more and loved better than most of us could dare to dream.

LIVING WITH A SAINT

In the beginning of this little book I said that I couldn't remember the first time I learned who Mother Teresa was, but that over time she had become an incresignly significant part of my life. That was certainly true, and, especially after my experience in college seminary, she became one of my "Go to Girls" when I needed some heavenly inspiration and intercession. I never expected, though, that one day Mother Teresa would literally reach out and touch me from Heaven, yet that's just what happened not very long ago.

I've been out of seminary now for more than ten years. I've gotten married, had two children and make my living writing, speaking, and giving parish missions and retreats. Fr. Bullock, the seminary rector who told me that great story about his encounter with Mother moved on, too. He's now the pastor of a large parish in Waterloo, Iowa. I was recently giving a mission at his parish, and he surprised me like I've never been surprised before or since.

At the end of the mission he recalled the story, but went on to tell that, though Mother had asked him to move to a different section of the chapel, she had come over and spent some quality time with him. Mother loved seminarians and young religious, and while her celebrity made her uncomfortable, she was willing to use it to encourage young vocations to the priesthood and religious life. At the end of their time together she signed her name to a prayer card she had given him. And there, at the end of that mission, in the church in Waterloo, Iowa, he gave that card to me.

Yes, the woman who has inspired me these many years with her life, story and example, showing me what it means to be a true disciple of Jesus Christ, reached out to me. I now have a real, tangible, physical item to connect me to one of my greatest teachers—a woman I have never met, but whom I know very, very well, and love very, very much.

So, as this little book comes to a close, I leave you with the prayer she left for Fr. Bullock, and, through him, for me. Pray it often and think of me, even as I think of you and all those who hear me talk and read what I write. And remember me, if you can, when you think of the

Little Nun of Calcutta, who even now in Heaven is reaching out with arms wide open for you in prayer.

Make us worthy, Lord, to serve our fellow men throughout the world who live and die in poverty and hunger.

Give them through our hands this day their daily bread, and by our understanding love, give peace and joy.

Amen.

To contact Jon for your next parish mission or event visit:

www.JonLeonetti.com

Made in the USA
Middletown, DE
26 September 2016